CRITICAL THINKING
—— IN ——
AMERICAN HISTORY™

Evaluating the Articles of Confederation

Determining the Validity of
Information and Arguments

Greg Roza

rosen
central™

The Rosen Publishing Group, Inc., New York

Published in 2006 by The Rosen Publishing Group, Inc.
29 East 21st Street, New York, NY 10010

First Edition

Library of Congress Cataloging-in-Publication Data

Roza, Greg.
Evaluating the Articles of Confederation: determining the validity of information and arguments/Greg Roza.—1st ed.
    p. cm.—(Critical thinking in American history)
Includes bibliographical references and index.
ISBN 1-4042-0413-X (lib. bdg.)
1. United States. Articles of Confederation. 2. Constitutional history—United States. 3. United States—Politics and government—1775–1783.
I. Title. II. Series.
KF4508.R69 2005
342.7302'9—dc22

                                                          2004027347

Manufactured in the United States of America

On the cover: Left: Philadelphia State House, Pennsylvania. Right: A map of the thirteen original colonies and the British possessions in Canada.

Contents

What Are the Articles of Confederation?

The Articles of Confederation, ratified by Congress in 1781, is a document that represented the first plan of government for the United States of America. It contains a preamble that introduces the document, and thirteen articles. The Articles of Confederation established a federal government that would bind the thirteen independent states together into a union. It remained the new nation's plan of government until 1789, at which point it was replaced by the U.S. Constitution.

The Articles of Confederation was first drafted and ratified by colonial leaders during the American Revolution (1775–1783). It reflected the colonists' need for a unifying federal government, but one that would not interfere in the businesses of the individual thirteen states. At the time, the

Word Works

✓ **confederation** The body formed by persons, states, or nations united by a single cause.

✓ **preamble** An introductory statement.

✓ **article** A single, numbered clause that is part of a larger document.

✓ **ratify** To formally approve.

Find a sentence in which each of these words appear in the text on pages 4–5. Use these words in new sentences of your own.

4

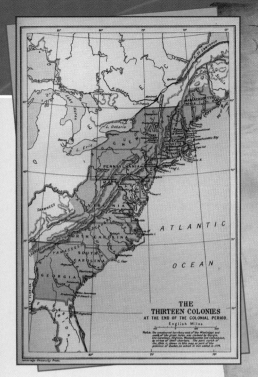

THE
THIRTEEN COLONIES
AT THE END OF THE COLONIAL PERIOD.
English Miles

colonists were at war with Great Britain, a country that controlled their commerce and international affairs while denying them certain freedoms available to British citizens. Many of the states were worried that a strong federal government would be too similar to the government against which they were rebelling. The amount of power given to the federal government became the subject of disputes over the Articles of Confederation.

A manuscript page from the Articles of Confederation appears above. It was adopted by the Continental Congress on November 15, 1777. Eventually it was ratified by all thirteen original states, which appear in the map above left.

The First Continental Congress

From September 5 to October 26, 1774, members of the First Continental Congress met in Philadelphia, Pennsylvania, to discuss what they believed was Britain's unfair treatment of its American colonies, including taxation without representation in the British parliament. The infamous Boston Tea Party occurred in 1773, in which Massachusetts colonists dumped British tea into Boston Harbor to protest tea taxes. In reaction, the Intolerable Acts were passed by the British parliament. These laws were designed to punish Massachusetts for its colonists' rebellious actions, and included such punishments as the closing of Boston Harbor and the restriction of the powers of the Massachusetts legislature.

Members of the Continental Congress maintained that the British parliament had no right to pass laws that affected the colonies, especially laws regarding trade and commerce. They also stated that each colony had the right to control its own business. The members of the congress agreed

Fact Finder

Have a look at these questions before you read this section. Look for answers to them as you read the text.

✓ For what purpose is the First Continental Congress held?

✓ What are the Intolerable Acts?

✓ What is the Declaration of Rights and Grievances?

On the night of December 16, 1773, a group of Boston colonists boarded three British ships loaded with East India Company tea. In a protest against tea taxes and the company's growing monopoly, the colonists dumped 342 chests of tea overboard.

to suspend all trade with Britain until Parliament repealed the Intolerable Acts. The congress also drafted a document titled the Declaration of Rights and Grievances, which listed the rights they demanded as colonists. They sent the document to King George III, and agreed to meet once again if he refused to address their grievances.

Even though its main purpose was to demand equality and fairness, not independence, the First Continental Congress was the earliest organized effort to loosen British rule over the colonies. The delegates discussed the right of each colony to control its own business without outside interference. Many of the ideas discussed in the First Continental Congress mirrored the ideas that would eventually provide the foundation for the Articles of Confederation.

The Beginning of the War

As the colonial leaders feared it would, the British parliament ignored the Declaration of Rights and Grievances. Britain considered the colony of Massachusetts to be in a state of rebellion. In order to contain this rebellion and prevent its spread, the British increased the pressure on all of the colonies instead of granting them representation in Parliament. This was a miscalculation, because the colonies responded with more protests. The result of all this rising tension was an outbreak of fighting on April 19, 1775, in the Massachusetts towns of Lexington and Concord. This marked the beginning of the American Revolution.

The colonists were not prepared for a war. They lacked weapons, supplies, leadership,

Paper Works

✓ Team up with classmates to write a newspaper article that persuades colonial citizens to take up arms against the British.

✓ Assign the following roles to students: researcher, writer, editor, typist, and readers.

✓ Present the facts while striving to raise interest in the cause.

✓ Use the library or Internet to back up the ideas presented in the text.

Ideas to think about as you research and write:

✓ The colonists lack resources, leadership, and manpower. What reasons can you give to persuade colonists to join the cause despite these disadvantages?

✓ Who is George Washington, and why should colonists trust him as a leader?

American colonists and British soldiers engage in battle in Lexington, Massachusetts, on April 19, 1775. The battles of Lexington and Concord were the first of the Revolutionary War.

an army, a navy, and a central government. This made it difficult to unite the colonists against the world's greatest empire, which was much better equipped for war. However, British reinforcements needed to travel a great distance and did not always arrive in time to bolster the British army. The patriots had a smaller army, but could raise new troops much faster than the British could, and thus were able to keep on fighting even soon after losses in battle. Led by great leaders such as General George Washington, the colonists were eventually able to win important battles, as in the victory in Saratoga, New York, in 1777. These victories helped to convince colonists as well as other countries—especially France—that the rebellious colonies could in fact win a war against the military giant, Great Britain.

Public Opinion

At the outbreak of the American Revolution, nearly two-thirds of the colonists were either Loyalists or they simply refused to take sides. Loyalists were colonists who remained supportive of the British king, George III, and wished to remain under British rule. Loyalists were often, but not always, wealthy merchants and landowners who were not greatly affected by British restrictions on colonial trade. Quakers, members of the religious group called the Religious Society of Friends, were also against the war because they were against violence of any kind. Quakers had a strong presence in New Jersey, Pennsylvania, Delaware, North Carolina, and Rhode Island.

Gradually, however, public opinion began to swing in favor of war. There were several reasons for

Get Graphic

Follow these directions to create a cause-and-effect graphic organizer.

✓ In the middle of a piece of paper, draw a large box labeled "effect."

✓ Draw four more boxes around the first box, each labeled "cause." Connect the four boxes to the middle box with lines.

✓ Write the following sentence in the box labeled "effect": Public opinion began to swing in favor of war.

✓ Use information from the text on pages 10–11 to fill in the cause boxes.

A mob forces a stamp officer to resign his post in this lithograph by famous illustrator Howard Pyle. After the passage of the unpopular Stamp Act, those officers charged with enforcing it and collecting the taxes were often subject to violent protests.

this shift. Businesspeople were angered by the increasingly harsh restrictions forced upon them by the British parliament. Patriotic propaganda caused many colonists to question the rights that they did and did not have. Early military successes made many colonists think, for the first time, that they might actually have a chance of beating England.

The Second Continental Congress

Even as the early battles of the Revolutionary War broke out across the colonies, colonial leaders began confidently planning for their eventual freedom. The Second Continental Congress met on May 10, 1775, in Philadelphia, Pennsylvania, to draft a list of laws that would serve as a constitution for the United States of America (as they began to call the union of independent colonies).

These brave leaders faced a difficult task. They wanted to avoid the kinds of government problems that ultimately led to the Revolution in the first place, but this caution often led to other problems. For example, most of the colonies were against a strong centralized government that would rule over the colonies. This was because they were presently fighting against a powerful king who controlled many aspects of colonial life.

Q & A

✓ For what reasons would some colonial leaders be in favor of a strong federal government?

✓ For what reasons would some colonial leaders be against a strong federal government?

✓ Had you been a colonial leader at the Second Continental Congress, would you be for or against a strong federal government? Explain your answer.

Some colonial leaders, however, recognized the need for a powerful central government to unify and strengthen the thirteen colonies as a whole.

In addition to signing the Declaration of Independence in the summer of 1776 (shown above), the Second Continental Congress was also busy at this time debating what form the government of the future United States should take. Its deliberations resulted in the nation's first constitution, the Articles of Confederation, which was adopted by Congress in 1777, and fully ratified in 1781.

Colonial leaders were in agreement that a definite plan of government was needed to oversee the states once independence from England was achieved. Yet the debate between state versus federal powers would develop into a major disagreement. This conflict would hinder the drafting and efficiency of the United States' first constitutional document, the Articles of Confederation.

The Lee Resolution

One of the colonial leaders present at the Second Continental Congress was Richard Henry Lee, a delegate from Virginia. The Lee Resolution, approved by the Second Continental Congress on July 2, 1776, reflected the recent shift in public opinion throughout the colonies. The simple yet powerful language of the resolution proposed three courses of action: the creation of a formal declaration of independence; the creation of a "plan of confederation," or constitution; and the establishment of alliances with foreign powers that might help the rebellious colonies in their fight against England.

These three ideas were soon fulfilled. On July 4, 1776, the Declaration of Independence, drafted by Thomas Jefferson, was approved by the members of the Second Continental Congress. On November 15, 1777, the Articles of Confederation was adopted by the congress. From 1776 to 1778, the colonists were secretly funded by France. In addition, France openly supplied the colonists with

Word Works

✓ **propose** To form or put forward a plan.

✓ **resolution** A formal expression of opinion voted on by an official body or assembled group.

✓ **alliance** An association between countries for the purpose of advancing the common interests of the members.

In June 1776, Thomas Jefferson drafted the Declaration of Independence *(above)* and submitted it for numerous revisions. Congress adopted the final version on July 4, 1776, and delegates began signing it on August 2.

weapons, supplies, and troops beginning in 1778. Spain and the Netherlands, allies of France united against their common enemy, England, also sent support to the colonists in 1779 and 1780.

Drafting the Articles of Confederation

The members of the Second Continental Congress felt that it was important to quickly draft a constitution. The war had begun, and there was a great need for unity between the states. The congress selected John Dickinson, a delegate from Pennsylvania, to head the committee to draft the first constitution of the newly formed United States of America.

The committee members decided that the document they were drafting had to address several key issues that were of great concern to many colonial leaders. The committee members did not want a single entity, group, or individual to hold too much power. Too much power given to one person or office might limit the rights of the states. Most delegates to the Second Continental

Fact Finder

Look for the answers to these questions as you read or reread the information in this section.

✓ Why did the members of the Second Continental Congress believe it was important to quickly draft a constitution?

✓ What key issues was the committee most concerned with when drafting the Articles of Confederation?

✓ What does "decentralized" mean?

✓ Use your answers to these questions to develop a larger essay on the influence of English colonial rule on the drafting of the Articles of Confederation and its principles.

John Dickinson, a delegate from Pennsylvania, served as chairman of the committee charged with drafting the Articles of Confederation, even though he did not yet support independence. The first draft, in Dickinson's handwriting, was submitted to the Second Continental Congress on July 12, 1776.

Congress were instead in favor of a form of government that was decentralized, or spread out over a number of regional governments. As a result, the committee members tried to create a flexible document that would respect the individuality of all the states, while at the same time creating a powerful union between them.

Disagreements Among the Thirteen States

The Articles of Confederation was submitted to the Second Continental Congress on July 12, 1776, eight days after the signing of the Declaration of Independence. However, the document was not adopted by Congress until November 15, 1777, and was not ratified by the states until 1781. This delay was due to several disagreements between the states. The smaller states did not want proportional representation in Congress. If more populous states could send more representatives to Congress than smaller states, the smaller states feared that their interests would be ignored and they would be pushed around. Similarly, the larger states did not want to have to pay taxes based on population, since they would end up paying far more than the smaller states would.

Paper Works

✓ Write two persuasive essays, one from the perspective of a small-state representative, another from the large-state point of view. Your audience is the Articles of Confederation drafting committee.

✓ Small-state representative—Write an essay persuading your audience that small states deserve representation in Congress equal to larger states.

✓ Large-state representative—Write an essay persuading your audience that large states deserve greater representation in Congress than smaller states.

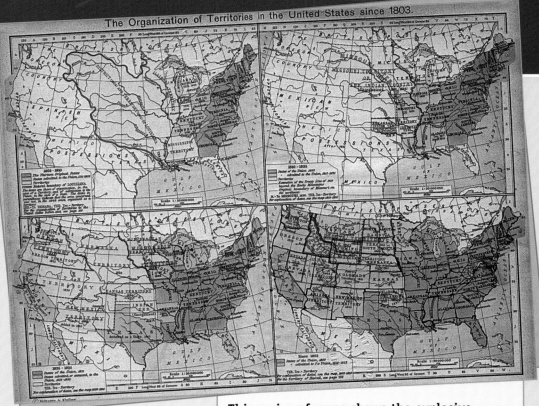

This series of maps shows the explosive growth of United States territory from 1803 to 1855. A key sticking point in the debates over the Articles of Confederation was the competition between frontier-bordering states and coastal states for control of the sale and development of frontier land.

In addition, states that did not border the unsettled frontier between the Appalachian Mountains and the Mississippi River wanted the federal government to control the sale of land so that all states could benefit from real estate profits. States that bordered on the frontier wanted to control as much of the unsettled land as possible. This would enable them to eventually extend their borders west and make money from the sale of the frontier land.

A Document Completed

On November 15, 1777, after much negotiation and bargaining, the Second Continental Congress adopted the Articles of Confederation as the first constitution of the United States of America. The preamble briefly yet boldly declared the freedom and independence of the thirteen states and listed each state as an equal partner in the new government. The thirteen articles of this document attempted to establish a favorable union between the states while safeguarding each state's individual rights and freedoms.

The three issues that had delayed certification of the articles—representation, taxation, and

Fact Finder

As you read or reread the information on pages 20–27, search for the answers to these questions.

✓ Which article declared that the thirteen states "entered into a firm league of friendship," and what exactly does that mean?

✓ According to the Articles of Confederation, on what criteria were voting and tax collection based?

✓ How many votes did each state receive in the federal government?

✓ How many states were needed to approve amendments to the Articles of Confederation?

the frontier—were each resolved.

The Articles of Confederation stated that voting and tax collection would be based on the value of buildings and land in each state and not on the population of each

state. The fourth article was designed to preserve a strong union between the states by promoting free travel between the states. Each state was granted only one vote in the federal government regardless of its physical size, population, or the number of representatives it sent to Congress. The document also specified that each state had an equal right to frontier territory.

State Powers

Article 2 of the Articles of Confederation declared that each of the states was a free, sovereign, and independent entity. It also declared that any power not specifically defined as a federal power in the subsequent articles was to be understood as a power granted to the state governments.

Article 6 listed the powers granted to the federal government and not given to the states. Most of these powers were related to foreign affairs and war. Article 6 prohibited (forbade) states from establishing their own embassies in foreign countries or meeting with foreign ambassadors. While states could maintain militias like those established during the Revolutionary War, they could not maintain a standing navy or army "unless such State be infested by pirates." No state could go to war with another state or foreign power unless it was at-tacked. A state was also not allowed to negotiate a spe-cial treaty with another state.

Word Works

✓ **sovereign** Self-governing and independent.

✓ **prohibit** To forbid something.

✓ **treasury** A governmental department in charge of raising, storing, and paying out money.

The word "sovereign" is an adjective that means "self-governing and independent." "Sovereignty" is a noun that means "freedom from external control."

French minister Conrad Alexandre Gerard de Rayneval (bowing and holding a tri-corner hat) is introduced to the Continental Congress on August 6, 1778. Under the Articles of Confederation, only the federal government—not individual states—could meet with foreign ambassadors and form alliances with foreign powers.

Article 8 said that a treasury would be maintained for the purpose of paying for a national military. The states were expected to pay taxes into this treasury in proportion to the value of all the land and property in the state. The taxes could be raised by any means each state deemed necessary. However, the Articles of Confederation did not give the federal government power to enforce the collection of state taxes, and many states simply refused to pay them.

Federal Powers

Even though the Articles of Confederation upheld the sovereignty of the states, it also stressed the importance of unity between the states. For example, Article 13 stated that "the Articles of this Confederation shall be inviolably observed by every State, and the Union shall be perpetual." Likewise, Article 3 declared that the thirteen states "entered into the firm league of friendship" that shared similar interests and a similar enemy.

Article 9 listed the specific federal powers granted to the United States Congress. Congress had the power to declare war, enter into treaties with foreign powers, and assign and send ambassadors to other countries. Congress could appoint officers to the army and navy and make the rules for those branches of the armed forces. The federal government could settle disputes between states, including disputes over land. Congress could borrow money, set up a post office, and charge postage. Congress could also control trade with Native Americans. A president of Congress was chosen by its members to preside over debates for a

Q & A

✓ In your own words, what does the following sentence mean? "The Articles of this Confederation shall be inviolably observed by every State, and the Union shall be perpetual."

✓ Why do you think the drafters of the Articles of Confederation decided foreign affairs should be handled by the federal government and not by state governments?

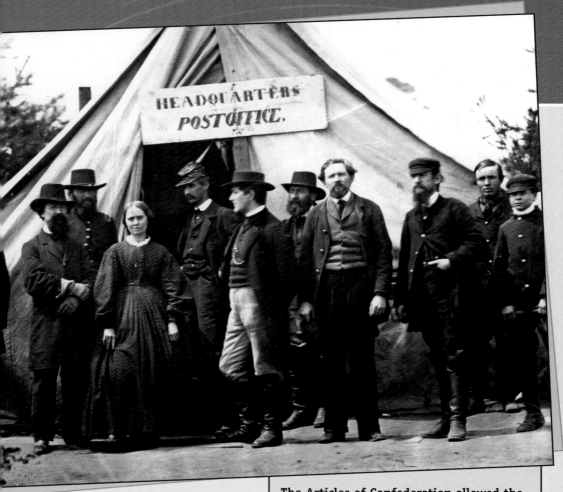

The Articles of Confederation allowed the federal government to operate post offices. This 1863 photograph shows a makeshift Union army post office in Falmouth, Virginia, during the Civil War.

term of one year, after which a new president was chosen.

Article 12 stated that the United States (meaning the federal government) was responsible for paying all colonial debts that had accumulated before the creation of the Articles of Confederation. Because the federal government could not force the states to pay taxes, however, it had difficulty collecting enough money to repay the new nation's debts.

Congress and Delegates

The fifth article of the Articles of Confederation defined the procedures that were to be followed in Congress. The members of Congress were to meet on the first Monday in November every year. Each state could send no fewer than two and no more than seven delegates to Congress. However, each state received only one vote in Congress regardless of the number of delegates it sent. Each delegate served for a single term of no more than three years. Articles 9 and 10 established the Committee of the States made up of one representative from each of the thirteen states. This committee made important decisions when Congress was in recess. The Committee of the States could only rule on matters designated by Congress, including borrowing money and raising and equipping an

Think Tank

Create a "congress" made up of your classmates. Assign students to one of the original thirteen states. Each state should have no fewer than two, and no more than seven representatives.

✓ Discuss and vote on the following three amendments to the class constitution:

1. There will be no running in the classroom.

2. The three states with the most representatives don't have to do homework.

3. The three states with the fewest representatives will get free ice cream on Fridays.

✓ Each state receives only one vote, no matter how many representatives it has.

✓ All states must vote in favor of the amendment in order for it to become a law.

✓ Were you able to pass any of the laws? Why or why not?

Between 1781 and 1789, Congress held sessions in Philadelphia, Pennsylvania; Princeton, New Jersey; Annapolis, Maryland; Trenton, New Jersey; and New York City. Above is the building used by Congress in Annapolis in 1783 to 1784.

army when necessary. Representatives could select a president for the committee who could serve for no more than three years. Proposals in Congress had to be approved by nine of the thirteen states in order to become laws.

Article 13 declared that Congress was the main governing body for all of the states. The Articles of Confederation was the new nation's first constitution and provided the country with its fundamental governing structure and foundation. So any proposed changes to it required careful thought and thorough debate. For this reason, all thirteen states needed to approve amendments to the Articles of Confederation before the amendments could be implemented. If just one state refused to vote for an amendment, the amendment would not be passed.

Weaknesses of the Articles of Confederation

The framers of the Articles of Confederation created a decentralized government that limited the power of Congress to intervene in what were seen as state matters. This was an attempt to create a sense of trust between American citizens and their new federal government. The sovereign states often showed little regard for the federal government and its oversight. The federal government could not regulate state trade, for example, and could not force the states to pay their taxes. The federal government was not even given sole power to coin money. Instead, each of the states coined its own money, which resulted in problems and confusion in commerce between the states.

It was difficult for Congress to make and enforce laws under the Articles of Confederation. Measures passed by Congress had to be approved by nine of the thirteen states, and amendments to the Articles of Confederation needed to be approved by all thirteen states. In many cases, states refused to approve new laws that did not serve their own interests. Even when Congress was able to pass laws, there was no federal court system in place yet to enforce them. It was up to the states to enforce federal laws, and they often lacked the interest or manpower to do so.

K-W-L

✓ Before reading the text of the K-W-L chart, study it. The first column has facts that you already **know** from reading this book. The second column has questions that you may **want** to discover. The third column will contain things you have **learned** from reading this section.

✓ Think about the chart as you read the text. When you are done, write answers to the questions posed in the "What Do I Want to Know?" column on a separate piece of paper.

What Do I Know?	What Do I Want to Know?	What Have I Learned?
The Articles of Confederation was designed to protect the sovereignty of the individual states.	Did ensuring the sovereignty of individual states harm the United States of America as a whole?	
The Articles of Confederation created a decentralized form of government.	What problems resulted from the establishment of a decentralized form of government?	
The Articles of Confederation intended for the states to "enter into a firm league of friendship."	Did the "league" of states always work together as a whole to settle problems?	

Shays's Rebellion

Most soldiers of the American Revolution were not paid for their wartime service, and they returned to their homes and farms penniless. Many Massachusetts farmers, in particular, were unable to pay the high taxes placed upon their properties. They then lost their farms and were sent to debtors' prison. Farmers sought to lawfully address these problems. Little was accomplished, however, and more and more farmers were stripped of their property and freedom. Soon, many of these farmers began to feel that revolt was their only option.

A full-scale rebellion began when Massachusetts farmers began barring entrance to courthouses to prevent the trials that sent their fellow farmers to debtors' prison. In 1787, Daniel Shays, a veteran of the

Paper Works

You are a veteran of the American Revolution and a Massachusetts farmer. Like many of your fellow farmers, you are in danger of losing your property and being sent to debtors' prison. Write a letter to your state government that is personal, descriptive, and issue-based.

✓ Personal: Begin the letter by introducing yourself and stating your profession and place of residence.

✓ Descriptive: After your introduction, describe your situation and outline the problems that led to it.

✓ Issue-based: Discuss the changes you believe the government needs to make to improve the lives of veterans and farmers like yourself.

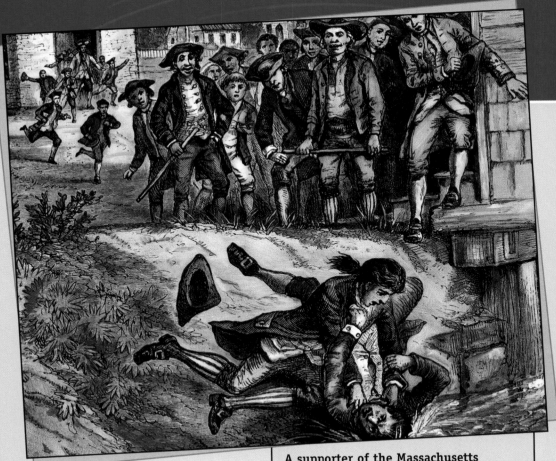

A supporter of the Massachusetts government and a rebellious farmer get into a fight during Shays's Rebellion in this undated illustration. Captain Daniel Shays was captured and later pardoned for leading the rebellion.

American Revolution and a farmer from Massachusetts, led an army of farmers in an attack on the U.S. arsenal in Springfield, Massachusetts. The farmers were defeated, but Shays's Rebellion helped to bring about change, nevertheless. Many political leaders who had led the revolt against England, including George Washington, Samuel Adams, and John Hancock, now realized that the Articles of Confederation did not grant the federal government enough power to address local or regional difficulties like those that led to Shays's Rebellion.

The Constitutional Convention

Shays's Rebellion is just one example of the negative effects the weaknesses of the Articles of Confederation had on the new and growing nation. In May 1787, delegates from twelve states met in Independence Hall in Philadelphia, Pennsylvania, to revise the Articles of Confederation. Rhode Island did not send a delegate because its citizens did not want the federal government interfering in their business. A majority of the delegates decided that a completely new plan of government was needed to unite the country and provide greater order. The document they decided to create became the U.S. Constitution. The members of the convention elected George Washington as the presiding officer.

While many of the delegates agreed that a new

Think Tank

Discuss the following questions with a small group of classmates. Take turns expressing your opinions and explaining your ideas.

✓ Do you think it was a good idea or a bad idea for Rhode Island to refrain from sending a delegate to the Constitutional Convention?

✓ Do you think the delegates of the Constitutional Convention should have rewritten the Articles of Confederation instead of writing a whole new constitution?

✓ Do you think the larger states deserve greater representation in Congress, since they have more land and more people?

✓ Did everyone in your group agree about the answers? Did the discussion change anyone's original opinion regarding the questions?

George Washington presides over the Constitutional Convention in Philadelphia's Independence Hall in 1787. The delegates from twelve of the thirteen states were charged with creating a "more perfect union" by revising the Articles of Confederation.

plan of government was needed, several key disagreements delayed the final decision. The larger, more populous states argued that they deserved greater representation in Congress, while the smaller, less populous states insisted on equal representation. Some delegates wanted a powerful federal government, while others demanded that the new document protect the rights of the states by creating a weaker federal government.

Federalists vs. Anti-Federalists

During the debate over the formation of a new constitution to replace the Articles of Confederation, two distinct sides emerged. Those in favor of a strong federal government became known as Federalists.

Some politicians still opposed the ratification of the U.S. Constitution, however. Those Americans became known as anti-Federalists. Many anti-Federalists agreed that the federal government was too weak, but they were more worried that the U.S. Constitution would grant the federal government too much power and open the door to tyranny. It was because of pressure from the anti-Federalists, however, that the Bill of Rights was added to the U.S. Constitution in 1791. These ten amendments to the Constitution spelled out the rights and freedoms of individual citizens that no one, not even the

Think Tank

Form a group of twelve students. Split the group evenly into Federalists and anti-Federalists. The rest of the class will form an audience.

✓ Both sides will be given an equal amount of time to discuss and present their view for or against the ratification of the U.S. Constitution to the audience.

✓ The audience will then be given time to discuss the two sides of the argument in preparation for a vote.

✓ Which side did the majority of your classmates vote for, the Federalists or the anti-Federalists? What argument or point was the most persuasive for them?

THE

FEDERALIST:

A COLLECTION

OF

ESSAYS,

WRITTEN IN FAVOUR OF THE

NEW CONSTITUTION,

AS AGREED UPON BY THE FEDERAL CONVENTION,
SEPTEMBER 17, 1787.

IN TWO VOLUMES.

VOL. I.

NEW-YORK:

PRINTED AND SOLD BY J. AND A. McLEAN,
No. 41, HANOVER-SQUARE.
M, DCC, LXXXVIII.

James Madison *(above left)*, along with Alexander Hamilton, called for a Constitutional Convention to revise the Articles of Confederation. A 1788 printing of Madison, Hamilton, and John Jay's pro-Constitution writings *The Federalist Papers* appears above right.

federal government, could violate or take away.

The formation of the Federalist and anti-Federalist groups was a continuation of the states' rights debate that had surrounded the Articles of Confederation. The Federalists and the anti-Federalists were merely two groups of politicians, each loosely composed of people who agreed on this one issue. Yet these two political camps eventually evolved into the first American political parties.

The U.S. Constitution and the Articles of Confederation

On September 17, 1787, after nearly four months of debating and revision, the U.S. Constitution was signed. This document is considered by many to be the fairest and most innovative plan of government ever penned. The Constitution defined the powers of the federal govern-

The U.S. Constitution, above, was signed on September 17, 1787, and took effect in 1789.

ment while protecting the rights of individual states and citizens. A side-by-side comparison shows the benefits of the Constitution over the Articles of Confederation.

Get Graphic

✓ Could Congress levy taxes under the powers of the Articles of Confederation?

✓ Which plan of government provided for a bicameral Congress?

✓ Under the U.S. Constitution, what steps are necessary to get amendments passed?

✓ Give three reasons the federal government is more powerful under the U.S. Constitution than under the Articles of Confederation.

Issue	Articles of Confederation	U.S. Constitution
Branches of federal government	Legislative (Congress)	Executive, legislative, judicial branches
Congress	Unicameral (a single body of lawmakers called Congress)	Bicameral (House of Representatives and the Senate)
Voting in Congress	One vote per state	One vote per representative, or senator
Courts	State-run; no federal court system	Each state has its own court system, but the Supreme Court hears important cases between states and individual citizens
Interstate trade	Congress had no power to regulate trade	Congress given power to regulate trade and collect taxes
Currency	Each state could coin its own money	Only Congress given power to coin money
Military	Congress depended on the states to raise forces	Congress given power to form national military
State representatives in Congress	One representative regardless of size, appointed by state legislatures	Number of representatives based on size of state, elected by popular vote; two senators appointed by each state legislature (changed in 1913 to a popular vote)
Amendments	When agreed upon by all states	When agreed upon by two-thirds of both houses and three-fourths of all states
Levying taxes	Congress could only ask states to pay taxes	Congress may levy taxes on individual citizens

The Legacy of the Articles of Confederation

The preamble to the Constitution begins with these words: "We the people of the United States, in order to form a more perfect Union . . ." The phrase "more perfect" is a direct reference to the weaknesses of the Articles of Confederation. Although the Articles of Confederation proved to be a flawed and ineffective plan of government, it still holds a position of importance in the history of the United States of America. Through its successes and its failures, America's first constitution helped to shape the country in the early years of its existence. The Articles of Confederation provided the country with a sense of stability during the American Revolution. Conflicts over the Articles of Confederation led to the birth of American political parties. They also gave the young nation a chance to experiment with and perfect a

Q & A

✓ Despite its failures, what were some of the strengths of the Articles of Confederation?

✓ Do you think the Founding Fathers could have written the U.S. Constitution had they not written the Articles of Confederation first? Explain your answer.

✓ Would the Constitution be the same today if the Articles of Confederation had not been the first plan of government in America? Explain your answer.

✓ Use your answers to these questions to develop a larger essay on the positive aspects of the Articles of Confederation and its long-term value to the development of the U.S. government, states' rights, and individual freedoms.

New York's Federal Hall appears above. Before the American Revolution, it served as City Hall and then housed the Continental Congress after the war. When the Constitution was ratified in 1788, New York City served as the nation's capital, and City Hall was remodeled and renamed. The drafting of the Bill of Rights and George Washington's inauguration occurred here.

fair and democratic government. American politicians wisely chose to abandon the Articles of Confederation in favor of a "more perfect" plan of government. But without that original constitution, America may not have evolved into the country that it is today.

Timeline

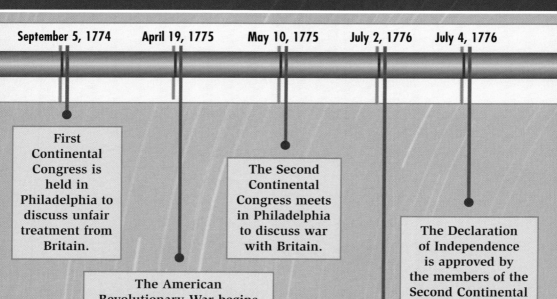

September 5, 1774   April 19, 1775   May 10, 1775   July 2, 1776   July 4, 1776

First Continental Congress is held in Philadelphia to discuss unfair treatment from Britain.

The Second Continental Congress meets in Philadelphia to discuss war with Britain.

The Declaration of Independence is approved by the members of the Second Continental Congress.

The American Revolutionary War begins when fighting breaks out between British and American forces at Lexington and Concord.

Get Graphic

Study the timeline to answer these questions.

✓ In what city did the Second Continental Congress meet to discuss war with Britain?

✓ Were the Articles of Confederation adopted before or after the end of the American Revolution?

✓ Which state did not send delegates to the Constitutional Convention?

Richard Henry Lee of Virginia introduces the Lee Resolution to the Second Continental Congress.

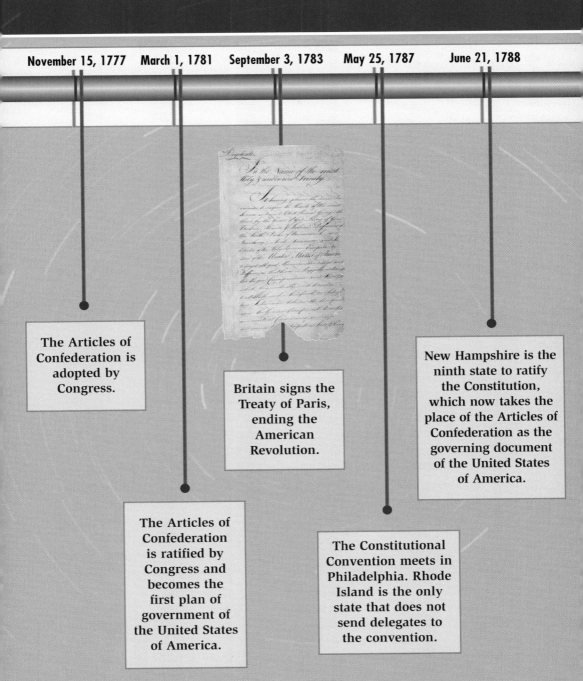

November 15, 1777   March 1, 1781   September 3, 1783   May 25, 1787   June 21, 1788

The Articles of
Confederation is
adopted by
Congress.

Britain signs the
Treaty of Paris,
ending the
American
Revolution.

New Hampshire is the
ninth state to ratify
the Constitution,
which now takes the
place of the Articles of
Confederation as the
governing document
of the United States
of America.

The Articles of
Confederation
is ratified by
Congress and
becomes the
first plan of
government of
the United States
of America.

The Constitutional
Convention meets in
Philadelphia. Rhode
Island is the only
state that does not
send delegates to
the convention.

Graphic Organizers in Action

Venn Diagram: Small States versus Large States

Large States

✓ Wanted greater representation in Congress

✓ Did not want taxes to be
based on population

✓ Wanted access to
frontier territory

✓ Wanted a decentralized
government with a weak
Congress

✓ Wanted to conduct
their own commer-
cial business

Small States

✓ Wanted equal
representation
in Congress

Main Idea/Supporting Ideas Web:

The Federalist Argument

Main Idea: A new plan of government was needed because the
Articles of Confederation created a weak federal government.

Supporting Idea: The
federal government had
little control over
American commerce.

Supporting Idea: It was
difficult for the federal
government to create and
enforce laws.

Supporting Idea:
The federal govern-
ment had no power to
regulate trade
between the states.
States set up their
own rules and taxed
other states.

Supporting Idea:
The federal government
did not have sole power
to coin money. Each
state coined its own
money, resulting in
problems in commerce
between the states.

**Supporting
Idea:** Each state
was given only
one vote in
Congress, and it
took nine out of
thirteen votes to
pass a law.

**Supporting
Idea:** There
was no federal
court system
to try federal
crimes.

Series of Events Chain: The events that
led up to the Drafting of the Articles of Confederation

Britain passes a series of tax laws to raise revenue in the colonies.

Colonists protest unfair British taxes.

Britain imposes even more taxes (which become known as the Intolerable Acts) and tighter military control on the colonies.

Britain ignores the colonists, and tensions continue to rise.

Colonial leaders hold the First Continental Congress to protest the Intolerable Acts.

Colonial protests increase in number and intensity.

The American Revolution begins on April 19, 1775.

The Articles of Confederation are drafted and adopted by the Second Continental Congress.

Get Graphic
Study the graphic organizers to answer these questions.

✓ The series of events chain shows the events that led up to the drafting of the Articles of Confederation. Can you create a chain showing the events that led up to the drafting of the U.S. Constitution?

✓ The Venn diagram compares and contrasts the viewpoints of the large and small states during the drafting of the Articles of Confederation. Can you create a diagram that compares and contrasts the state and federal government powers after the ratification of the Articles of Confederation?

✓ The main idea/supporting ideas web shows the Federalist argument for the revision of the Articles of Confederation. Can you create a web displaying the anti-Federalist view?

Glossary

adopt (uh-DOPT) To accept formally and put into use.

ambassador (am-BA-suh-dor) Someone who represents the official viewpoint of his or her home country in a foreign country.

bicameral (bi-KAM-er-uhl) Relating to a single legislature made up of two chambers, such as the U.S. Congress's House of Representatives and Senate.

confederation (kon-fed-uh-RAY-shun) The act of coming together to form a league of nations, or the league of nations itself.

constitution (kahn-stih-TOO-shun) The principles and laws of a nation or state that detail the government's powers and duties, and the rights of citizens.

decentralized government (dee-SEN-trul-iyzd GUH-vern-mint) A nation that has power spread out over a large number of regional governments, rather than one powerful, central government.

delegate (DEHL-uh-git) A person representing a large body of people, such as a state.

embassy (EM-buh-see) A body of diplomatic representatives or ambassadors, as well as the building in which they work.

federal (FEH-duh-rul) Relating to a central or national government rather than individual or state governments.

grievance (GREE-vuns) A complaint, often in a written format.

legislature (LEH-jis-lay-chur) A lawmaking body.
patriot (PAY-tree-ut) Someone who loves his or her country, strongly supports its interests, and works for its continued existence.
ratify (RA-tih-fy) To formally approve, as in a law.
sovereign (SAHV-rin) Self-governing and independent.
unicameral (yoo-nee-KAM-uh-rul) Relating to a legislature with only one chamber.

Web Sites

Due to the changing nature of Internet links, the Rosen Publishing Group, Inc., has developed an online list of Web sites related to the subject of this book. This site is updated regularly. Please use this link to access the list:

http://www.rosenlinks.com/ctah/evac

For Further Reading

Burnett, Betty. *The Continental Congress: A Primary Source History of the Formation of America's New Government*. New York, NY: The Rosen Publishing Group, Inc., 2004.

Callahan, Kerry P. *The Articles of Confederation: A Primary Source Investigation into the Document That Preceded the U.S. Constitution*. New York, NY: The Rosen Publishing Group, Inc., 2003.

Feinberg, Barbara Silberdick. *The Articles of Confederation: The First Constitution of the United States*. Brooklyn, NY: Millbrook Press Inc., 2002.

Freedman, Russell. *In Defense of Liberty: The Story of America's Bill of Rights*. New York, NY: Holiday House, 2003.

Hossell, Karen Price. *The Articles of Confederation*. Chicago, IL: Heinemann Library, 2003.

Hossell, Karen Price. *The United States Constitution*. Chicago, IL: Heinemann Library, 2003.

Hull, Mary E. *Shays' Rebellion and the Constitution in American History*. Berkeley Heights, NJ: Enslow Publishers, 2000.

Index

About the Author

Greg Roza has a bachelor's and a master's degree in English from the State University of New York at Fredonia. He has been writing history and science books for young students since 1999. He has written several books for the Rosen Publishing Group on colonial-era history, politics, and government. Greg has a wife named Abigail, a daughter named Autumn, and a son named Lincoln.

Photo Credits: Cover (left), pp. 23, 25, 27, 31, 33, 35 (left) © Bettmann/ Corbis; cover (right), pp. 5 (left), 19 © Perry-Castañeda Library Map Collection/Historical Maps of the Americas/ The University of Texas at Austin; pp. 5 (right), 9, 13, 15, 21, 35 (right), 36, 40, 41 © National Archives and Records Administration, Washington, DC; pp. 7, 11 © Bridgeman Art Library; p. 17 © Stapleton Collection/Corbis; p. 39 © MPI/ Getty Images.

Designer: Nelson Sá; Photo Researcher: Nelson Sá